The journey is long
Much strength is needed

To reverse the cycle
That has preceded.

Poetry by
LAWRENCE HOO

CARGO

Foreword
Charles Golding

At the root of CARGO is the search by Lawrence Hoo for the answers to two questions that have long dominated his consciousness. The first is how subtle and persistent racism experienced by Britain's West Indian communities—the often called African Diaspora—has limited their life chances and subjugated them to poorer living standards, higher incidences of crime, and other negative social factors. The second is how Lawrence could redress the consequences of this racism so his children may have access to all the privileges and opportunities that life in Britain has to offer its citizens.

The resultant body of work, CARGO, inspires hope, encouragement, and empowerment by providing a much-needed narrative that sets out the accomplishments of a people with a legacy of enslavement, who overcame the pervasive obstacles of racism.

When Lawrence reflects on growing up in Bristol in the '70s and '80s, he feels that this exclusion and marginalisation is due to history being taught from a solely European perspective, and that this has devalued other cultures and achievements, especially those of African communities impacted by slavery.

References to ‘the dark continent’ or a ‘savage land full of uncivilised and uneducated Africans’ has robbed generations of their dignity, self-esteeme and self-worth. This insidious approach has limited people’s horizons, influenced thinking, and continued oppression within mainstream society.

Lawrence believes that the system that enables Europeans to excel is skewed to ensure the failure of Africians and the people of the African Diaspora, and that this directly influences policing policies. Stop and search disproportionately affects Africian Caribbean communities leading to a greater likelihood of arrest, detainment, and eventually criminal records. The everyday incidents in which African Caribbean people pass others in the street, who interpret their presence as a threat, only compound this perception of subjugation.

Lawrence remembers being followed in shops as an eight-year-old—clearly under suspicion—and feeling undermined and undervalued by hyper-vigilant shopkeepers. It is small wonder that he adopted an anti-authoritarian stance in response to his anger at an inescapably negative and disempowering environment.

It was rage that encouraged him to write his first poem. In 2003, against a backdrop of conflict and tension in St Pauls', Bristol, a Jamaican dealer assaulted Lawrence's partner and child causing Lawrence to retaliate. Whilst reflecting on the extremes he was prepared to go to protect his family, Lawrence wrote *Life* using words instead of violence to address his situation.

Lawrence is adamant that the thoughts, actions and behaviours of people from all backgrounds must change for people from Africa and of the African Diaspora to be recognised as strong, resilient, competent, and equal.

Central to this change is to challenge the presentation of the Transatlantic Slave Trade: its impact, its legacy, and the way it is spoken about, written about and taught in schools. Historical and contemporary examples of the skilfulness, inventiveness, and craftsmanship of both Africans and the people of the African Diaspora must complement this teaching. In this way, the cultural contributions of Africans and the people of the African Diaspora will begin to gain the standing they deserve.

Life

To all the people shopping at the Mall
Going to purchase something big or small

Do you really know about our life?
Living where drugs and vice are rife?

Let me open your eyes to the life we live
Don't worry, I'm not gonna ask you to give

Just listen

When I walk the streets with my eyes wide open
These are the things I see that need to be spoken

Crackheads, smackheads, and hoes loitering on the street
Perverts, punters, and police circling the beat

Round and round their lives continually spinning
Can you tell me out of this game, who is winning?

Who really cares about all this pain?
Who is really responsible and what do they gain?

If you listen to the news they make it all sound so plain
It's the Yardies that bring the drugs over sea by plane

Have you ever thought they didn't bring this disease?
Maybe it's the authorities that brought our community to its knees?

But

Could you imagine if we all had the same opportunity in life?
We might all end up happily married with three kids and a wife

See these are the things that surround our children day by day
When they go to schools, shops or just out to play

The children have to learn how to survive while all around is evil
How can the authorities say they treat us all the same, as equal?

In Conversation
John Akomfrah & Lawrence Hoo

John Akomfrah CBE was first introduced to Lawrence Hoo by DJ and producer Goldie at the offices of Smoking Dogs Films in 2004. At this time Hoo was on the verge of publishing his first book, *Inner City Tales*, and shared excerpts from his planned documentary of the same name. This work captured the troubled nature and the narrative of events occurring around his hometown of Bristol.

Hoo's reflection on the culture of the African Diaspora and the importance of artistically capturing historical record fairly, combined with his uncompromising vision, left a lasting impression on Akomfrah with the pair having met several times since. More recently, Hoo introduced a new body of his work, known at the time as *Shipshape and Bristol Fashion*.

'These new poems focus on the achievements of people from the African Diaspora; the revolutionaries and activists responsible for change, and their own achievements, rather than those of the European abolitionist movement.' Hoo goes on to explain further, 'There is a responsibility, a legacy, handed down from those ancestors, to empower those affected by the African Diaspora.'

The new collection struck Akomfrah as a 'bold and impressive call to arms', with aspirations aligned with his own work and endeavours—'For many years, people have tried to communicate the story behind the Transatlantic Slave Trade but have failed to change the nature of the address.' Since then, there has been work on a multimedia interpretation of Hoo's poetry collection, now known as CARGO.

'If you wish to occupy the multiple zones of poetry, visual art and political history, you need to realise each of the zones has its own demands. CARGO answers those requirements in a unique and engaging way,' Akomfrah says. Many artists similar to Hoo have approached traditional institutions for support in creating African historical, cultural and artistic initiatives and have not received the help they needed. 'Their conventional imperatives are to say no to narratives of this type,' Hoo says, reflecting on his past.

Born from this belief, Hoo decided to separate himself from traditional systems and increase the versatility of his project by using new methods to express himself and his work.

With huge rewards on offer
and so much to gain

Ships continued to sail
in search of fortune and fame

Edward Colston is held as the beacon
for this trade

When the reality is that through it
Bristol was made

In turn, this provided the opportunity to create an interesting and immersive space filled with multimedia sensory experiences relating to his poems.

'I'm always looking and thinking about where new narratological devices could come from—and who's thinking of them,' says Akomfrah. CARGO employs the latest audio-visual techniques to tell the stories in Hoo's work, allowing him to physically guide the audience through history and into the present day.

'It's a sensorial experience,' says Akomfrah. The poetic nature of CARGO's installation, coupled with Hoo's verse, is designed to inspire a new perspective, perception and attitude towards the way the Transatlantic Slave Trade has been taught for so long.

Akomfrah believes that CARGO genuinely feels different. 'It's interesting and compelling—and if seen by the right people, stands a chance at having a real cultural and sociological significance.'

Hoo turns to reflect on his hometown, 'Bristol has always had a problem around it's involvement with the Slave Trade. People want to address it in some way but they don't know how; by failing to significantly alter the nature of our approach we haven't yet helped this cause.'

Akomfrah has a passion and a commitment to documentary. He realises the importance of capturing a historical record and understands that a surplus of fictitious narratives often have a habit of working their way into the sociological mix. Akomfrah says 'there is often a societal amnesia that needs to be combated, preventing the kind of forgetting that builds into a hierarchy where there are beings and non-beings.'

'CARGO is deeply rooted within Hoo's personal experiences and conveys his need to communicate his own historical truth. This stands out amongst an ever-prevailing climate of indifference,' says Akomfrah. 'We all need the ballast of memory and history to counterbalance the ever prevailing tides of false truth.'

In response to this, Hoo states 'my aim is to combat the situation with an intellectual approach as opposed to a visceral, violent and reactionary approach.'

The union of Hoo's poetry and the multimedia installation formed around it creates a bold cultural proposal that attempts to create a new narrative space for itself, African history, and those works that will follow it.

REVOLUTION
ACTIVISTS
CHANGE

ROUTES

A way or course taken in getting from a starting point to a destination

Shipshape and Bristol Fashion

Shipshape and Bristol Fashion
Is the mantra of this great city
Whose ships sailed the seas
With unbridled passion

Venturing out in search of lands unknown
Not knowing if they will ever return home

With huge rewards on offer and so much to gain
Ships continued to sail in search of fortune and fame

William de la Founte is recorded as the first to get paid
Through navigating Bristol a route into lucrative Portuguese
trade

In 1497 John Cabot returned from new found land
Kickstarting the era in which Bristol became grand

A few years later William Weston is credited with finding more
routes that were new
Due to these endeavours the stature of the City of Bristol
expanded and grew

Bristol's Merchant Venturers asked the King for his blessing and
a royal charter
The King agreed, giving Bristol his backing and the power to
barter

Bristol's ships circumnavigated the globe enabling trade that
was before untold
Bristol's Merchant Venturers gained great wealth from new
cargo being sold

And through taking hold of the reigns for the running of the city
They allowed Bristol to reap the rewards from all the nitty gritty

Navigating Bristol's fortunes through the winds of change
Laying down foundations for a city about to rearrange

William de la Founte, John Cabot and William Weston are
Bristol's trading pioneers
The trinity who established the routes that nourished Bristol
for hundreds of years.

John Cabot (c. 1450–c. 1500)

The Bristol Trade

Bristol built Colston's Hall a new extension clad in gold
Which reminded me of all the African Souls Bristol brought
and sold

Edward Colston is hailed as the beacon for this trade
When the reality is that through it Bristol was made

The city profited in so many ways
To name them all would take us days

Trade, commerce and stature is to name just a few
Of how through the African people's suffering Bristol grew

It was called the Slave Trade
So the people who profited could say gains were legally made

But if we were able to talk to Milosevic, Pinochet or Hitler
They would say the same even though we know their regimes
were sinister

What Hitler did was rightly called the Holocaust
Shouldn't the same be said for Africa when you see all she lost?

Through persecution, beatings, fear and death
People were enslaved till their last breath

People were taken from all over the great continent never
to return
And over time many would forget everything they did ever learn

Imagine not being allowed to speak in your native tongue
Imagine not being allowed to educate your young

Then over time your ways are lost and your history is forgotten
You become part of a world where you belong at the bottom

How was it possible for people to absorb such pain?
How could they witness such horrors and not go insane?

These are just a few of the things they had to endure
So that the people who made it legal could gain more

The people who did it said they were the civilised race
They keep rewriting history to make their case

But if we look at the facts and facts alone
Who was uncivilised and savage is easily shown.

Freedom and self-determination should be everyone's birthright

Throughout the Transatlantic Slave Trade there were people who knew it wasn't right

It is taught that freed slaves and abolitionists set the enslaved free

But what about all the enslaved that fought to overcome their captivity?

Edward Colston (1636–1721)

ROUTES

ACTIVISTS

CHANGE

REVOLUTION

A forcible overthrow of a government or social order, in favour of a new system

Warrior Queen

Freedom and self-determination should be everyone's birthright
Throughout the Transatlantic Slave Trade there were people who knew it wasn't right

Nanny was one such person, a freedom fighter who fought for this cause
Because she knew that people were being enslaved under unjust laws

Nanny was from the Ashanti people in Africa
Where women were treated with respect
Under British rule in Jamaica
They were enslaved, raped and hung by the neck

Nanny was taken from Africa to Jamaica and enslaved into this barbaric regime
But Nanny escaped and set out on her quest to make freedom more than just a dream

Nanny joined the Maroons, known for their fighting skills and bravery
Africans and Indigenous people who had escaped Spanish rule and slavery

Nanny was an amazing woman with exceptional leadership qualities
Which Nanny used to develop and establish new Maroon communities

Nanny planned raids on plantations which set the enslaved free
They would then join with the Maroons showing strength in unity

Due to these actions Britain declared war on the Maroons in 1720
The plan was to destroy the Maroon communities and force them back into slavery

Nanny was a military leader, a true warrior queen
Who used tactics against the British they had never seen

The Maroons would camouflage themselves to look like trees
Which enabled them to ambush the British soldiers with ease

The British suffered many losses due to the Maroons' superior combat skills
No matter how hard they tried they couldn't remove the Maroons from the hills

In 1739 the Maroons were offered a peace treaty to bring the war to an end
The British realised they couldn't win the war and would rather be the Maroons friend

Some Maroon leaders signed the peace treaty to end the war
Nanny refused because she didn't agree with this new law

The peace treaty gave the Maroons their own land but slavery remained legal
Nanny could never agree to sign anything that still allowed this evil

Nanny leaves a legacy that should be an inspiration to all
Of what can be achieved when your back's against the wall.

Nanny (1686–1755)

Independence Day

It is taught that freed slaves and abolitionists set the enslaved free
But what about all the enslaved that fought to overcome their captivity

There is so little recorded to explain this
Making it almost look like they lived in bliss

This could not be further from the truth
If they did not obey they'd be hanging from a noose

But their pride, strength and unity was too strong
To allow others to keep them enslaved for too long

Throughout the entire period of this legal trade
Enslaved Africans fought for their freedom till the grave

Their most triumphant battle was in Haiti
Where after a 13 year war they became free

Dutty Boukman started the rebellion after a spiritual ritual
That galvanised their strength and focused their will

Then Jean-Francois, Biassou and others carried it on
Until Toussaint Louverture and Jean-Jacques Dessalines ensured
they won

On January 1st 1804 Haiti declared itself an independent nation
Did this have any bearing on Britain's 1807 law of abolition?

Even though Haiti had become free
Many more were still bound in slavery

Unable to decide or plan for themselves
While being tormented in this living hell

Of being subjected to the will and desires of others
Who beat, killed and raped sisters and mothers
As well as all others from fathers to brothers
Through a hierarchy defined by colours

The true brutality that was served and dished out
Was too horrendous to be recorded or talked about

The lynchings and burnings were seen as a family outing,
a community event
But the raping, sodomy and torture was how the slavers
would silently vent

Through implementing this brutality as a show of power
They believed it would make the enslaved forever cower

But to their horror and ultimately their demise
The will for freedom would always uprise.

Independance Day (1st January 1804)

Samuel Sharpe (1801–1832)

Rebellions and revolutions
forced the hands of time

Bringing forward an end
to this most abhorrent crime

In life we have people
who give their all for others

Like the unconditional love
children receive from their mothers

Christmas Uprising

Rebellions and revolutions forced the hands of time
Bringing forth an end to this most abhorrent crime

For centuries the enslaved had been fighting for their freedom
While all from them was stolen by colonisers building a new kingdom

Samuel Sharpe was born in the Parish of St James, Jamaica in 1801
In the turbulent times just before slavery's days were meant to be done

Samuel Sharpe grew up to be an inspirational Baptist preacher
Who gained great status as an abolitionist anti-slavery speaker

Delivering sermons for freedom to his congregation
Preaching slavery must fall with no more segregation

Samuel Sharpe believed in God and the good in men
Due to his faith he felt he could summon them

To not fight but to stand for this just cause
To resist by peaceful protest, breaking unjust laws

After many meetings and debates it was finally agreed
That action must be taken if they were ever to succeed

Christmas 1831 Samuel Sharpe chose to start his peaceful protest
When the sugar cane was due to be cut so it would create much unrest

The peaceful protest began with strikes on plantations all
across Jamaica
Causing the plantation owners to get whipped up into a state
of hysteria

Word quickly spread that the protest had begun
A warship was called in to lay aim with its gun

Soon the situation exploded and grew out of hand
As people fought for their freedom in a stolen land

10 days the uprising lasted with over 60,000 of the enslaved involved
Fighting for their freedoms believing their actions should be absolved

In the aftermath Samuel Sharpe and over 500 others were brought
to account
Many sentenced to be hung, their heads cut off and placed
on a mount

The brutality of the punishments served had an escalating effect
It highlighted slavery's barbarism while undermining intellect

The abolition movement used the uprising to further their cause
It helped to accelerate the introduction of new anti-slavery laws

In 1833 the Abolition Of The Slave Trade Act was finally passed
Marking a victory for all who had laid down their lives in slavery's past

'I would rather die on yonder gallows than live my life in slavery'
Is the last Will and Testament to Samuel Sharpe's spirit and bravery.

ROUTES

REVOLUTION

CHANGE

ACTIVISTS

A person who campaigns to bring about political or social change

Mother Seacole

When I ask most people to name a famous nurse from history
Florence Nightingale is remembered while Mary Seacole is a mystery

Mary Seacole was a pioneering nurse and heroine of the Crimean war
Who achieved so much it's surprising that we weren't taught more

Mary Seacole was born in Kingston Jamaica in 1805
At a time when slavery was still very much alive

Mary Seacole was not born enslaved she was born free
Which enabled Mary Seacole to create her own destiny

Mary Seacole learnt nursing skills at the hands of her mother
Who showed her that nature had many healing properties to offer

This knowledge of nature's healing properties came from African traditions
Which had been passed down from parent to child for many generations

Mary Seacole used this knowledge to treat lots of illnesses and diseases
From cholera, yellow fever and malaria to just common sneezes

In 1854 Mary Seacole traveled to England to ask to join the British Army to serve as a nurse in the Crimean war
The War Office refused her requests to join, due to their prejudice, they believed her skills would be poor

Mary Seacole faced many obstacles due to her race and gender
But her will to help others meant that she would never surrender

Mary Seacole funded her own trip to the Crimea and set up a
boarding house to help the sick
From this base Mary Seacole would go onto the battlefield to
treat soldiers who needed help quick

Mary Seacole become known as Mother Seacole by British
soldiers in Crimea
They were so grateful for all her help and were always glad to
see her

When the war was over Mary Seacole returned to England,
where she was awarded several medals for her bravery
These stand as a record of what she achieved as a free woman,
instead of living a life bound in slavery

In life we have people who give their all for others
Like the unconditional love children receive from their mothers

Mary Seacole was one such person who fitted this mould
That is why her story deserves to be told.

You can shackle the hands
You can shackle the feet
You can imprison the bodies

But you cannot shackle
or imprison the minds

Is the truth
Marcus Garvey gave us
to unshackle our BINDS

Based on skill, determination, strength and willing

People would prove their worth and start winning

Mary Seacole (1805–1881)

Father Garvey
Marcus Garvey (1887–1940)

Father Garvey

Marcus Mosiah Garvey Jnr was born on 17th August 1887 in
St Ann's Bay, Jamaica
Throughout his life he fought against inequality, making him
a true chain breaker

From an early age Marcus Garvey's quest for knowledge was
plain to see
As he pored over books in his father's library, which became
his nursery

Submerged in books Marcus Garvey soaked up much knowledge
Being mostly self-taught, his father's library became his college

Marcus Garvey left school at age 14 to work as a printer's
apprentice
Which led to him leading a strike for higher wages and fighting
against injustice

These are the foundations that inspired Marcus Garvey to found
the United Negro Improvement Association
His goal was to unite the African Diaspora so they could work
together to rebuild their great nation

Self-determination was Marcus Garvey's ultimate goal
Being able to self-determine was his essence, his soul

The UNIA was the vehicle Marcus Garvey created to drive his
plans into reality
Quickly expanding across America and beyond, the UNIA soon
gained notoriety

Within a month of being established the UNIA had over two million members
Three years later it had grown to over 11 million, and this created uncomfortable tremors

Newspapers, property businesses and an emerging shipping line
Had the government and authorities determined to fit a crime

New laws were introduced to track and monitor Marcus Garvey's movements
In the hope of reversing his cause and the African Diaspora's improvements

J Edgar Hoover employed the FBI's first African American informant
Who he used to infiltrate and spy on Marcus Garvey's movement

In 1923 Marcus Garvey was sentenced to five years in prison for committing suspected mail fraud
It was hoped this would halt his rise, and propaganda was spread that his methods were flawed

Marcus Garvey was released from prison after serving two years of his sentence
Immediately returning to Jamaica to continue educating people was his insistence

Marcus Garvey's influence was still strong and in 1928 he created the People's Political Party
Which was the first political party to defend the interests of Jamaica's African Caribbean community

Marcus Garvey's will to deliver more than just hope for his people
Was unquestionable and rarely have we seen an equal

After ensuring the stability of the PPP
Marcus Garvey travelled to England to spread his philosophy

Never forgetting who he was and who he represented
Marcus Garvey would go to Speaker's Corner to address all
who attended

On the 10th June 1940 Marcus Garvey died at the age of 53
Leaving behind a wealth of knowledge for others is his legacy

He taught us to believe in one's self and one's worth
instead of feeling enslaved on a scorched earth

You can shackle the hands
You can shackle the feet
You can imprison the bodies

But you cannot shackle or imprison the minds

Is the truth
Marcus Garvey gave us
to unshackle our BINDS.

Windrush Generation (1940–60)

Ships Over Troubled Waters

I would like to tell you a story of how a journey was taken
By many people who were invited but were then forsaken

Please come and help! All are welcome! Jobs galore!
As long as you are prepared to be part of our underclass and poor

No No No No No—this isn't quite true
And if it was, do you think they'd tell you?

They invited you to come here to live and help rebuild their country
But didn't want you to live near or share in any new found prosperity

Rooms to rent but there are conditions applied
No Irish, No Blacks, No Dogs are allowed inside.

Can you imagine the confusion so many must have felt?
Answered a call of distress and were prepared to help

The warm reception they were offered was never received
It was obvious from the beginning that they had been deceived

Hostile receptions were the norm in that day
No rooms to rent even though you're able to pay

The inner city of Bristol suffered much damage during the war
And this became home to the city's underclass and poor

Many of the properties were derelict the rents were high
With choices few and far between, who could afford to ask why?

New arrivals from the Caribbean settled in and this created a new community
That was built on the foundations of cultural interests, protection and unity

St Paul's was the area that many would call home
It sits at the centre of Bristol's inner city zone

From this centre people would see each other on a regular basis
Allowing people to go from being strangers to regular faces

As the community grew problems were still evident
Number one being racism that was still prevalent

Exclusion was often the order of the day
When it came to getting a job or a place to stay

So many opportunities were offered but failed to materialise
So many people feeling rejected after being sold a pack of lies

But these obstacles weren't going to keep people held back
Especially as the main reason was being classed as black

Based on skill, determination, strength and willing
People would prove their worth and start winning

Winning the battle to create a life and home in a new country
Instead of accepting the life of the disempowered ethnic minority

On any journey of discovery you have great pioneers
Who put all on the line for the betterment of their peers

For you some of them I would like to list
So we can remember who did assist

Assist in enabling people to have a choice
Assist in enabling people to have a voice

They are true pioneers who faced many obstacles and broke new ground
For all that they did they deserve to be remembered and we should all feel proud

Malcom X, Martin Luther King, and Nelson Mandela are widely known
But what about the champions of Bristol, our own home grown

Roy Hackett
Delores Campbell
Owen Henry
May Tanner
Jim Williams
Olive Osborne
Barbara Dettering
Guy Reid Bailey
Princess Campbell
And Carmen Beckford to name just a few
Of the pioneers who came to England

We salute you.

ROUTES

REVOLUTION

ACTIVISTS

CHANGE

An act or process through which something becomes different

Carmen Beckford (1928–2016)

Fighting against injustice,
racial hatred
and for people's civil rights

They are modern day heroes,
the equivalent
of medieval knights

As we achieve through standing on the shoulders of all those who stood before us

We must continue this legacy for all those who trusted as well as lost trust

Our Festival Queen

I would like to pay tribute in honour of Carmen Beckford, a truly inspirational Jamaican woman
Whose faith and self-belief were instrumental in developing race relations in Great Britain

Carmen Beckford was born in St Thomas Jamaica on December 21st 1928
Did people imagine back then; that this new life's achievements would be so great?

After leaving Jamaica for Great Britain at the age of 17
Carmen Beckford settled in Kent in pursuit of her dream

Carmen Beckford's dream of a career in nursing became reality
Because of her work ethic, dedication and tenacity

In 1965 Carmen Beckford moved to Downend in Bristol to work as a midwife
Continuing on a journey of self-development that would be her calling in life

Later that year Carmen Beckford became Bristol's first race relations officer and an executive member, of the Commonwealth Co-ordinated Committee
As a founding elder, Carmen Beckford was committed to improving the lives and opportunities of people regardless of their ethnicity

Amongst these many appointments Carmen Beckford set up and ran the Bristol West Indian Dance Troupe
'Amazing, beautiful, elegant and strong, she was Superwoman to me', recalls one of the group

In 1968 St Paul's Festival was created with Carmen Beckford in charge of entertainment
This event still goes on today delivering unparalleled cultural interaction and social development

Carmen Beckford faced many challenges from within and outside her community
While working towards breaking down racial barriers for better cultural unity

Carmen Beckford wasn't one to turn away in the face of adversity
Carmen Beckford faced it head on, composed and eloquently

Due to Carmen Beckford standing firm in the face of much racial tension and abuse
Carmen Beckford was able to help people, who it was written in the script should always lose

Creating opportunities that would have otherwise been out of reach
Which enabled people to live, work, learn, grow and teach

Through perseverance, single-mindedness and self-motivation
Carmen Beckford's achievements were recognised by the nation

In 1982 Carmen Beckford received an MBE, an honour of the greatest order
From the ruling system that when established was set up to ignore her

Carmen Beckford was a leader, teacher, scholar and social activist
That reminds me of Angela Davis but less militant, more of a pacifist

Fighting against injustice, racial hatred and for people's civil rights
They are modern day heroes, the equivalent of medieval knights

Carmen Beckford shone a light so bright that the darkness had to lift
Coupled with her faith in God and self-belief, this was her greatest gift.

Marvin Rees (1972–)

Brother Marvin

As we achieve through standing on the shoulders of all those
who stood before us
We must continue this legacy for all those who trusted
as well as lost trust

Marvin Rees is one such person who had much to bear
After becoming Europe's first African Caribbean Mayor

Marvin Rees was born in Bristol in 1972 at the height of the UK's
Sus Laws
When incarcerating African Caribbean men due to suspicion was
a just cause

The signs in the windows that greeted Marvin's father on his
arrival had all disappeared
Racism was now hidden from plain view while still being
confronted daily and feared

Being born of a Jamaican father and English mother was not
widely accepted
It was looked down on by many, leaving families feeling shunned
and rejected

The inner city of Bristol became a safe haven for the African
Caribbean community
This is where Marvin's family settled as it offered them a sense
of belonging and security

But even within this community
Marvin was a member of a new minority

Who were classed as half-breeds or half-caste
Which could have you classed as an outcast

Growing up in the inner city of Bristol also exposed Marvin to
the extreme divisions of wealth and opportunity within the city
Just a mile away there was another life where crime wasn't
permitted; the streets were kept clean and the houses looked
pretty

The inner city streets of Bristol were neglected and suffered from
numerous acts of crime
That corrupted children before they had an understanding of life
resulting in many doing time

Marvin's mother's care, love and affection is a clear reflection on
the direction Marvin took in life leading to his election

Marvin took a route that steered him away from the streets
This resulted in him striving for and achieving great feats

Marvin learned discipline from an early age through joining his
local boxing gym
Along with attending church this installed faith, self-belief and
what it takes to win

Through these disciplines Marvin focused his will to excel and
create change
Believing life's injustices were unjust and that he could work to
break the chains

Graduating from several universities, including gaining a
fellowship from Yale
Marvin progressed instead of accepting the stereotypes that had
him labeled to fail

Marvin moved on to work for the BBC, the NHS and Labour Party
Fuelling his passion to work towards a City that is equal and free

Marvin has stayed true to this cause
And now reaps the rewards
Of following his dreams
As all can be more
Than at first it seems

Marvin Rees was elected Mayor of Bristol on the 5th of May 2016
Marking an incredible achievement for one who followed a dream

Now Marvin Rees's legacy has truly begun
A son of Bristol who became Europe's number one

Hibiscus Queen

If fairy tales were real then this would be one
Of how a descendant of the enslaved became a queen's number one

With our heroine's roots firmly planted in slavery
This is a tale of courage, endurance and bravery

Peaches Golding's journey is remarkable and unique
Chronicled through a history; dark, light, rich and deep

This branch of the family tree started with the sale of Bethania
in 1858
Bought to work as a housekeeper on the Hauser's 3000 acre estate

To have one ancestor who is purchased by another
Who becomes your matriarch, your eternal mother

While the other becomes your great-great-grandfather
Created a family tree that was hard to decipher

Over the next hundred years Peaches Golding's ancestors gained
social standing and independence
Showing in the stand taken by her father with his brave act
of defiance

Peaches Golding's father Charlie Hauser, was arrested for refusing
to move to the back of the bus in 1947
He was not prepared to accept his fate, and took out a case against
the Greyhound Bus Company for racial discrimination

This groundbreaking case which Charlie Hauser won resulted
in an apology and $2000 compensation
Heralding a victory against racial segregation 8 years before
Rosa Parks' refusal to stand inspired a nation

Crossing classes and cultures for the betterment of us all
Peaches Golding is driven to help the dispossessed stand tall

In recognition of this Peaches Golding was awarded an OBE
in 2009
Which started her ascent to a position none before had been able
to climb

In her presence you get an essence of the gift she shares
With sincerity in her eyes you can see that she cares
With an illuminating soul it is love that she bares

Peaches Golding was appointed High Sheriff of Bristol in 2010
Appointed to a position usually held by men

With being only the second of African descent
Peaches' spirit and beliefs inspire her ascent

Passionate, positive, dignified and regal
Is a legacy to aspire to, to stand as her equal

Peaches Golding's legacy is born from a journey of loss and
reconciliation
Which resulted in Peaches Golding being appointed to represent
a nation

Peaches Golding was appointed Her Majesty's Lord-Lieutenant
of the County and City of Bristol on April 22nd 2017
Making Peaches Golding Bristol's very own Queen
Which is a reality for us to know so we can continue to dream.

Peaches Golding (1953–)

Cleo Lake (1979–)

Passionate, positive,
dignified and regal

Is a legacy to aspire to,
to stand as her equal

Africa is where our journey started;
it's where humanity began

It's the birthplace of the ancestors
of every woman and man

Queen of Hearts

'Out of many we can be one Bristol'
Is the truth Cleo Lake wishes to instil

To some this seems like an over optimistic dream
But remember we all come from the same stream

Africa is where our journey started; it's where humanity began
It's the birthplace of the ancestors of every woman and man

We have many cultures and languages that set us apart
Yet we are all one and Cleo holds this in her heart

Cleo came to life from a cultural entwining
Two cultures, both human, no dividing

Growing up in Bristol Cleo faced a city divided
Where options presented were so one-sided

Race, wealth, and class were the elephants in the room
Propelling some to stardom while dragging others to doom

Driven by her desire to achieve
However hard Cleo had to believe

Believe in herself and her love for humanity
Which allowed Cleo to hold on to her sanity

Moving forward Cleo would still get knocked down
But she would find the strength to swim not drown

A mother, carnival leader, green councillor and Lord Mayor
Cleo Lake's ascession is a joy to share

Along her journey, much Cleo has learned
A knowledge gained that's duly returned

With having no fear of entering new spaces
Cleo Lake is connecting unsuspecting faces

Pulling together Bristol's cultural community
Breaking barriers down, rebuilding unity

Critically tackling Bristol's political elite
Creating a lake for our streams to meet.

ANTI
SOCIAL
SOCIAL
CLUB

Artist Statement
Lawrence Hoo

CARGO is a collection of poems written to create an inspiring narrative about people linked by African decent and Bristol.

Growing up in Bristol, I was surrounded by the achievements and exploits of the city of Bristol during the Transatlantic Slave Trade.

These narratives of glory and achievement are reinforced across statues, buildings, and institutions throughout the city. My ambition as a poet is to challenge this perception by bringing to life the hidden stories, the struggle and success, and the impact of the African Diaspora on Bristol throughout this 500-year period in history.

My hope is that through these poems people will gain a better understanding of the African Diasporic experience and how they fought for, thought about, and eventually wrought change. The city of Bristol now has Europe's first Mayor of African Caribbean descent, voted into office in 2016 by the people of Bristol, whose ancestors at the beginning of this journey would have classified him as property, as CARGO.

Thanks

I would like to thank my children, for without them none of this would have been possible. They are my inspiration, my guiding light.

Special Thanks
Arts Council England
Asher Craig
Chaz Golding
Clare Reddington
Festival of Ideas
Fiona McInnes-Craig
Hello Charlie
John Akomfrah CBE
Laura Marshall
Nema Hart
Rebecca Scott
Thresholds
Tom Morris
University of Bristol
Victoria Forrest

Thanks
Alec Stevens
Alex Briggs
Andrew Kelly
Andrew Samuels
Angie Bual
Anndeloris Chacon
Beaula McCalla
Bristol Old Vic
Carmen Beckford MBE
Cecil Walker
Chloe Meineck
Cleo Lake
Clive Smith
Colin Watson
David Haylock
David Punter
Desmond Brown
Dick Penny
Eleanor Pender
Emma Nuttall
Euella Jackson
Gary Thompson
Glens Kitchen
Grant Marshall
Halotronica
Heather Marks
Hilary O'Shaughnessy
Icon Films
Jade Maximen
Jasmine Creusson
Jason Mullins
Jimmy Galvin
Jo Kimber
Joyann Boyce
Junior Sheik
Kim Randal
Kuumba African Arts and Community Centre
Liam Wiseman
Lily Green
Lottie Donovan
Luke Emery
Lynn Mareno
Lyrically Justified
Mandy Rose
Marcus Gilroy Ware
Michael Jenkins
Molly Roff
MTM Awards
Neil Maggs
Nicola Hogg
Paul Tigwell
Peaches Golding OBE
Pervasive Media Studio
Philip Walker
Ras Judah Adunbi
Rima Mahdi
Rise Awards
Roger Griffith
Rosanna Dias
Ruby Osunsola
Sandra Gordon
Sharon Clark
Stephanie Mitchell
Stewert Jackson
Tarim
Tony Watson
Tristan Cork
Tyrone Maximen
Ujima Radio
Urban Word Collective
Verity Macintosh
Victoria Tilloston
Vyleen Maximen
Watershed
Waterstones
White Crate
Will Taylor
Zahra Ash-Harper

Lawrence Hoo is a celebrated poet and activist. He is the author of *Inner City Tales* (2006) and *Hoostory* (2011). *Hoostory* was exhibited at Centrespace Gallery (2007), The Drum, Birmingham (2008), and Wilder Street Gallery (2011). *Inner City Tales* documentary was screened at The Watershed (2006). Hoo uses his poetry to campaign against and challenge social imbalances, leading community creative writing courses and workshops. Hoo was Ujima Radio's Poet in Residence (2016), and received a RISE Award for Arts, Community and Entertainment (2018), and the MTM Award for Music, Arts and Culture (2018). Hoo lives and works in Bristol.

Charles Golding is a Senior Creative at UK design agency Hello Charlie. He has vast experience in creating exceptional live visuals for shows like the BRITs and the MTV awards, as well as working on projects with creatives such as Kanye West to David Attenborough. He has spearheaded global digital campaigns for the likes of the UN Refugee Agency to raise awareness of the issues faced by refugees around the world. Golding has a passion for creativity and collaboration, working with platforms that range from print to augmented reality.

John Akomfrah CBE is an award-winning Ghanaian-British artist, filmmaker, writer and cultural theorist. He is one of the founders of the Black Audio Film Collective (BAFC), a group of artists and filmmakers active between 1982 and 1998, dedicated to examining issues of Black British identity through film and media. Akomfrah made his debut as a director with *Handsworth Songs*, which won the Grierson Award for Best Documentary in 1987. In 1998 he co-founded Smoking Dogs Films, with Lina Gopaul and David Lawson, and has since pursued an individual and distinguished film practice, gaining him a high level of respect for his documentaries and films dealing with issues of race, identity and post-colonial attitudes. Akomfrah was a Governor of the British Film Institute (2001–07), Film London (2004–13) and is currently a trustee of the Tate Gallery (2015–present).

First published in an edition of 500 by
Inner City Tales
info@innercitytales.com
lawrencehoo.com

Creative Director: Charles Golding
Editor: Emma Nuttall
Reprographics: XY Digital
Print: Graphicom
Design & Production: Victoria Forrest
designbyvictoria.com

British Library cataloguing-in-publication data. A catalogue record of this book is available from the British Library.

ISBN: 978-0-9554015-2-7